KT-394-226

Flora's Big Noise

Written by Karen Wallace
Illustrated by Lisa Williams

WAYLAND

GLOUCESTERSHIRE COUNTY LIBRARY	
993238889 0	
PETERS	12-Nov-2008
	£8.99

Flora's Big Noise

First published in 2008
by Wayland

Text copyright © Karen Wallace 2008
Illustration copyright © Lisa Williams 2008

Wayland
338 Euston Road
London NW1 3BH

Wayland Australia
Hachette Children's Books
Level 17/207 Kent Street
Sydney, NSW 2000

The rights of Karen Wallace to be identified as the Author
and Lisa Williams to be identified as the Illustrator of this Work have
been asserted by them in accordance with the Copyright, Designs
and Patents Act, 1988.

All rights reserved

Series editor: Louise John
Cover design: Paul Cherrill
Design: D.R.ink
Consultant: Shirley Bickler

A CIP catalogue record for this book is available from the British Library.

ISBN 9780750254045

Printed in China

Wayland is a division of Hachette Children's Books,
an Hachette Livre UK Company
www.hachettelivre.co.uk

Flora the Elephant sometimes played a game with her friends.

The game was called 'Sneaking Up in the Jungle'.

Spots the Leopard was good
at playing 'Sneaking Up in
the Jungle'.

He walked through the trees so
softly that he didn't break a twig.

It was fun sneaking up on the other animals and surprising them!

Monty the Monkey was good, too.

He went swinging through the trees
so quietly that he didn't shake
the branches.

Lulu the Parrot was very good
indeed at playing 'Sneaking Up in
the Jungle'.

She landed on the bushes
as lightly as a fly.

Flora wasn't very good at the game.

She was just too big
and too heavy.

When she walked, she made too much noise.

When she blew through her
trunk, it sounded like a strong
wind blowing!

"Let's play our game," said Monty. "We can sneak up to the river. When we get there, we can all go swimming."

Spots laughed. "Great idea! We can surprise the frogs. It's fun to watch them jump in the water."

"Will you play with us, Flora?"
asked Lulu.

20

But Lulu knew that Flora didn't really like the 'Sneaking Up' game.

Flora shook her head.

"No thanks," she said. "But I LOVE swimming. I'll wait for you down by the river bank."

"I wish I wasn't so noisy," thought Flora sadly as she plodded through the jungle.

When she came to the river,
she sat down and looked out
at the water.

Suddenly, Flora saw a crocodile
hiding under a log. She knew
that crocodiles liked to gobble up
other animals!

Flora had to save her friends!
She blew through her trunk so
loudly that all the leaves rattled
on the trees.

At that moment, Monty, Spots and Lulu rushed out of the bushes. "What's the matter, Flora?" they cried.

Then Monty spotted the crocodile.
"Look!" he shouted.

Just in time, Flora had stopped
them all jumping into the water.

"Hooray for Flora the Elephant!"
cheered her friends.

"Flora's big noise has saved
us all!"

Flora laughed. "It's not so bad
being noisy after all!"

START READING is a series of highly enjoyable books for beginner readers. They have been carefully graded to match the Book Bands widely used in schools. This enables readers to be sure they choose books that match their own reading ability.

The Bands are:

Pink / Band 1
Red / Band 2
Yellow / Band 3
Blue / Band 4
Green / Band 5
Orange / Band 6
Turquoise / Band 7
Purple / Band 8
Gold / Band 9

START READING books can be read independently or shared with an adult. They promote the enjoyment of reading through satisfying stories supported by fun illustrations.

Karen Wallace was brought up in a log cabin in Canada. She has written lots of different books for children, fiction and non-fiction, and even won a few awards. Karen likes writing funny books because she can laugh at her own jokes! She has two sons and two cats. The sons have grown up and left home but the cats are still around.

Lisa Williams did her first drawing at 15 months old – it was a worm! She told her mum to write 'Worm' underneath the picture. When she was five, she decided that she wanted to be an illustrator when she grew up. She has always loved drawing animals and hopes that you will enjoy this book...